YO
WED
PLANNER

In the same series:
Getting it right: Wedding Speeches
Getting it right: The Best Best Man
Getting it right: Wedding Etiquette

YOUR WEDDING PLANNER

Carole Chapman

foulsham

London . New York . Toronto . Sydney

ACKNOWLEDGEMENTS

I should like to thank the following for their kind assistance in the preparation of this book: General Register Office, my friends and colleagues.

foulsham
Yeovil Road, Slough, Berkshire. SL1 4JH

ISBN 0-572-01761-8

Printed in Great Britain
by Cox & Wyman Ltd, Reading

CONTENTS

INTRODUCTION

Approximately 350,000 weddings take place each year in England and Wales. It seems that marriage is still very popular!

A wedding is a serious ceremony, a celebration, a public performance and a personal experience not to be entered into lightly. Love, romance and ritual make this mysterious and magical event one of the most exciting and memorable experiences of life.

Everyone enjoys a wedding, but the essential extensive planning and preparations can seem to be unduly daunting for the unwary bride and her family. Spontaneous weddings, spur-of-the-moment flings with all the family organising the celebration in a few weeks prior to the big event have declined and generally todays weddings are often planned and arranged twelve months or more in advance.

This book will help you to plan, prepare, and consider the options available, and provides practical guidance about all that a wedding entails.

ENGAGEMENT

When the bride-to-be has replied'Yes' to the all important question 'Will you marry me?', she then has the right to name the day.

The word 'fiancé' relates to the groom-to-be, 'fiancée' refers to the bride-to-be.

INFORMAL ANNOUNCEMENT

Taking the trouble to visit the bride's father (traditionally he was asked for his consent) is still one of the best ways of establishing an amicable son-in-law/father-in-law relationship.

Both sets of parents should be informed as soon as possible. They should be the first to learn of the news.

Do not announce your forthcoming marriage at someone else's wedding!

FORMAL ANNOUNCEMENT

Engagement parties are sometimes held where the father of the bride-to-be makes the official announcement of the engagement.

Forthcoming marriages may be formally announced in the newspapers.

> Mr S South and Miss/Ms N North The engagement is announced between Sam, only son of Mr and Mrs Sidney South of Southton and Nel, youngest daughter of Mr and Mrs Nigel North of Northton
>
> **or**
>
> A marriage has been arranged (and will shortly take place) between Mr Samuel South, son of ... of ... and Nel, daughter of ... of ...

The parents of the bride-to-be, or the bride, should send the announcement to the editor of the chosen newspaper (national or local) a few weeks beforehand, stating the date on which the announcement is to appear and including a daytime telephone number in case of queries. If a full address is included in the announcement, many circulars from advertisers of wedding services may follow.

On country farms where bees are kept, it is customary to tell the bees of the forthcoming marriage and to give them some wedding cake! Well-wishers should congratulate only the groom - women are not to be congratulated but wished every future happiness.

ENGAGEMENT RING

There is no necessity for the bride-to-be to have an engagement ring, but if desired, its design can take any form. It does not have to be a diamond.

In return for the engagement ring, it is usual for the bride-to-be to give her betrothed an engagement gift , such as a gold chain, tie clip, or signet ring.

Superstition
Fiancées' birthstones are said to be luck-bringers in engagement rings.

BREAKING THE ENGAGEMENT

If an engagement is broken by the bride-to-be, etiquette demands that she immediately returns the ring together with any gifts she has received from her fiancè. If the groom-to-be breaks off the engagement, his betrothed is entitled to keep the ring.

<u>*Superstition*</u>
This superstition relates to the first letter of the bride's surname:
Change the name and not the letter - you'll marry for worse and not for better.

<u>Month</u>	<u>Birthstone</u>	<u>Symbolizes</u>
January	Garnet	Constancy
February	Amethyst	Sincerity
March	Bloodstone	Courage
April	Diamond	Purity
May	Emerald	Happiness, hope
June	Pearl, agate	Prosperity, health
July	Carnelian, ruby	Fidelity, passion
August	Sardonyx	Bliss
September	Sapphire	Wisdom
October	Opal	Hope,
November	Topaz	Companionship
December	Turquoise, Lapis lazuli	True contentment, harmony

NAME THE DAY, DATE AND MONTH

Legally you may marry on any day (except Christmas Day) between 8am and 6pm. Jewish weddings can take place at any hour.

Register offices are closed on Saturday afternoons and on Sundays.

Spring and summer weddings are usually the most popular.

<u>*Superstition*</u>
The month of May is considered bad luck.
Marry in May, rue the day!
Marry in May, unhappy for Aye!

<u>*Superstition*</u>
Married on a:
Monday, brides will be healthy;
Tuesday, brides will be wealthy;
Wednesday, brides do best of all;
Thursday, brides will suffer losses;
Friday, brides will suffer crosses;
Saturday, brides will have no luck at all.
It is considered unlucky to marry on a Friday
especially on Friday 13th!

LEGAL REQUIREMENTS

MINIMUM AGE

A marriage solemnised between persons either of whom is under the age of 16 is void.
Persons of either sex under the age of 18 need the legal premission of their parents or guardians to marry.

RELATIONS WHO MAY NOT MARRY

A marriage solemnised between persons within certain degrees of relationship is void.

For men	For women
Mother	Father
Adoptive mother or former adoptive mother	Adoptive father or former adopted father
Daughter	Son
Adoptive daughter or former adoptive daughter	Adoptive son or former adoptive son
Father's mother	Father's father
Mother's mother	Mother's father
Son's daughter	Son's son
Daughter's daughter.	Daughter's son
Sister	Brother
Father's sister	Father's brother
Mother's sister	Mother's brother
Brother's daughter	Brother's son
Sister's daughter	Sister's son

Note: A 'brother' and 'sister' include a brother or sister of the half-blood.

Marriage is prohibited between persons within certain degrees of affinity, unless certain conditions are met.

For men	For women
Daughter of former wife	Son of former husband
Former wife of father	Former husband of mother
Former wife of father's father	Former husband of father's mother
Former wife of mother's father	Former husband of mother's mother
Daughter of son of former wife	Son of son of former husband
Daughter of daughter of former wife	Son of daughter of former husband

The conditions under which any marriage within the above degrees of affinity is permissible are that both parties to the marriage have attained the age of 21 at the time of the marriage and that the younger party has not at any time before attaining the age of 18 been a child of the family (i.e. a child who has lived in the same household as that person and been treated by that person as a child of his family) in relation to the other party.

In addition, marriage to the parent of a former spouse is prohibited unless both parties to the marriage have attained the age of 21 and both the former spouse and the other parent of the former spouse are dead when the marriage is solemnised. Marriage to the former spouse of a son or daughter is similarly prohibited unless both parties to the marriage have attained the age of 21 and both the son or daughter and other parent of the son or daughter are dead when the marriage is solemnised.

A valid marriage may be contracted between a man and a woman who is the sister, aunt, or niece of a former wife of his (whether living or not), or was formerly the wife of his brother, uncle, or nephew (whether living or not). This applies also where the kinship is of the half-blood. However, a marriage is not valid if either party is at the time of the marriage domiciled in a country outside Great Britain which does not recognise its validity.

Legal Requirements For Marriage In England And Wales

The following notes outline the legal requirements for marriage in England or Wales. Further information may be obtained from any Superintendent Registrar or from the General Register Office in London. Throughout these notes, Superintendent Registrar is abbreviated to 'SR'.

Preliminary formalities

1   Before a marriage may take place in
     England or Wales, there are certain
     preliminary formalities that the law
     requires to be observed. These fall into two
     categories:

     Civil.
     These must precede every marriage in a
     register office or according to any religious
     faith other than the Church of England (see
     paragraphs 2-8).

     Ecclesiastical.
     A marriage in the Church of England may
     take place after certain civil preliminaries
     (see paragraphs 2-5), but it is more usual
     for the marriage to follow banns or a
     licence by the Church authorities (see
     paragraphs 15-17).

Superintendent Registrar's Certificate Without Licence

2   If both parties reside in the same
     registration district, each party must have
     lived within that district for seven days
     immediately preceding the giving of the

notice. Notice must be given to the SR of that district and may be given by either party.

3   If the parties reside in different districts notice must be given to the SR of each district. Each party may give notice in his or her district or either party may give both notices. However, notice cannot be accepted until both parties have lived in their respective districts for the seven days immediately preceding.

4   The building in which the marriage is to take place must be specified in every notice of marriage. It must be in the district of residence of the parties, or of one of them, but there are certain exceptions to this if the marriage is to take place other than in a register office.

5   Twenty-one clear days must intervene between the day on which the SR enters the notice in his notice book and the day on which he issues his certificate. The marriage may then take place within three months from the day on which the notice was entered.

Superintendent registrar's certificate and licence

6   Both parties must be in England or Wales
      or must have their usual residence in
      England or Wales on the day the notice is
      given. Only one notice is required whether
      the parties reside in the same or different
      registration districts and the notice may be
      given by either party. One of the parties
      must have resided in the registration district
      in which notice is to be given for 15 days
      immediately preceding the giving of the
      notice and the marriage must (with the
      exceptions referred to in paragraph 4) take
      place in that district. If both parties have
      resided for 15 days in different districts, the
      notice may be given to the SR of either
      district but the marriage must take place
      (with the exceptions mentioned in
      paragraph 4) in the district in which such
      notice is given.

7   The building in which the marriage is to
      take place must be specified in the notice.

8   One clear day, other than a Sunday,
      Christmas Day or Good Friday, must
      intervene between the day on which the SR
      enters the notice in his notice book and the

day on which he issues his certificate and licence. The marriage may then take place at any time within three months from the day on which the notice was entered.

Marriage in special circumstances

Marriage of House-bound and Detained Persons

9   Enables marriage between parties, of whom one is either house-bound or a person detained as a prisoner or mental patient, to be solemnized on the authority of a SR's certificate without licence at the residence of the party who is house-bound or detained.

10   Notice of marriage must be given as set out in paragraphs 2-5. Further information can be obtained from the SR who will also explain what evidence is required to meet the statutory conditions.

11   The marriage may be solemnized according to the rites of the Church of England, by such other religious ceremony as the parties choose (other than according to the usages of the Jews or the Society of Friends) or by civil ceremony.

Marriage by Registrar General's Licence

12   Where a person who is seriously ill and not expected to recover and is too ill to be moved to a register office or registered building, the Registrar General may grant a licence for the marriage to be solemnized in the place where the patient is lying.

13   Notice of marriage must be given personally by one of the parties to the SR of the district in which the marriage is to be solemnized, who will explain what evidence is required. There is no waiting period before the licence may be issued.

14   The marriage may be solemnized by civil ceremony or according to the rites of a denomination other than the Church of England, or according to the usages of the Jews or the Society of Friends. (For marriage in such circumstances according to the rites of the Church of England see paragraph 17.)

Marriage according to the rites of the church of england

15   A Church of England marriage may be solemnized after any of the following preliminaries:

i   the publication of the banns;

ii   the issue of an ecclesiastical licence (in these notes referred to as a common licence);

iii   the issue of a special licence granted by or on behalf of the Archbishop of Canterbury;

iv   the issue of a SR's certificate.

16   Questions relating to marriage according to the rites of the Church of England are a matter for the Ecclesiastical Authorities. Further information is available upon application to the clergyman of the church in which it is desired that the marriage shall take place.

Banns

17   Application for the publication of banns should be made to the clergyman of the parish in which each party resides. Banns must be published on three Sundays before the marriage can take place.

The Church authorities advise that a marriage in a church of the Church of England between two foreigners or between a foreigner and a British subject should be by licence and not after banns.

Common Licence
This exempts the parties from the necessity of banns.

Special Licence
Issued only in grave emergencies or very exceptional circumstances and enables a marriage to be solemnized according to the rites of the Church of England at any time and place.

Superintendent Registrar's Certificate
A marriage according to the rites of the Church of England may be solemnized on the authority of a certificate of a SR instead of after the publication of banns. In such case:

i the conditions set out in paragraphs 2-5 apply. In addition, note that, with certain exceptions, one of the parties must have the required residence in the parish or ecclesiastical district in which the church or chapel where the marriage is to take place is situated. Further, the place of residence and the church or chapel must be within the registration district of the SR to whom notice is given;

ii   the marriage may not be solemnized
        without the consent of the clergyman of the
        church or chapel in which it is desired it
        shall take place or by any person other than
        a clergyman of the Church of England;

iii   the notice to the SR takes the place of the
        publication of banns - there cannot be
        publication of banns in respect of one party
        and the issue of a SR's certificate for the
        other party.

General information

Fees

18   Civil preliminaries - details are available
        from SRs.

19   All parishes in the provinces of Canterbury
        and York - derived from the table of fees
        issued by the Church Commissioners.
        Details can be obtained from the minister.

Giving Notice

20   Where notice of marriage has to be given to
        a SR it should, whenever possible, be given
        to that officer direct. For the convenience
        of the parties however, notice may usually
        be attested on personal attendance before
        any Registrar of Births, Deaths and

Marriages for the district in which the party giving the notice resides. The notice so attested may then be sent by post or otherwise to the SR but the party giving the notice is responsible for the cost of transmission and must take the risk of delay or loss in transit. The notice is held not to have been duly 'given' until it has been received by the SR and entered in his notice book.

Consent to the Marriage of a Minor

21 The consent of parents or other lawful guardian(s) of a person under 18 years of age must first be obtained and it should be produced in writing when notice of marriage is given to a SR. The fact that such consent has been obtained forms a part of the declarations which are made when the notice of marriage is given or when application is made for a common or special licence. If the parents or guardians are abroad their signatures to the consent should be properly witnessed, preferably by a notary or a Consular Officer. When the marriage is to be solemnized after the publication of banns and the parent or other lawful guardian openly declares in the

church or chapel, at the time of the publication, his dissent from the marriage, the publication of banns will be void. A marriage may not take place between persons either of whom is under the age of 16.

Objections to a Marriage

22   If any circumstances are alleged which, if true, would invalidate a notice of marriage, or if any caveat has been entered, the issue of the licence or certificate may be delayed until the allegation has been satisfactorily met by the party who gave the notice.

Production of Documents

23   If the birth certificates of the persons getting married are readily available it is helpful to the SR if they can be produced to him when notice of marriage is given. In the case of a marriage involving a person from abroad, an official travel or identity document for that person should be produced.

All persons who have been previously married should also produce documentary evidence of the death of the former spouse or of the dissolution or annulment of the marriage.

Photocopies of the documents are not acceptable without certification.

Witness

24 The parties to the marriage must arrange for the attendance of two witnesses to be present at the marriage and to sign the marriage register.

Marriage Certificate

25 A certified copy of the entry recording the marriage may be obtained at the time of marriage.

One Party Resident in Scotland

26 Where one of the parties lives in Scotland and the other in England or Wales a marriage may take place in England or Wales in a registered building, a register office or according to the usages of the Society of Friends or the Jews, on production of a SR's certificate in respect of the party living in England or Wales and a Scottish registrar's certificate of no impediment in respect of the party living in Scotland. For information as to the procedure to be followed by the party

resident in Scotland, application should be made to the Registrar General, General Register Office, New Register House, Edinburgh EH1 3YT.

27 A marriage in England or Wales in a church or chapel of the Church of England or the Church in Wales may be solemnized after banns or by common licence or, with the consent of the officiating clergyman, on production of a SR's certificate in respect of the party living in England or Wales and a Scottish registrar's certificate of no impediment in respect of the party in Scotland.

Marriage in Scotland

28 The party resident in England or Wales may obtain a SR's certificate for production to the registrar in Scotland, or may give notice to the registrar in Scotland, either in person or by post. It is recommended that, about six weeks before the date of marriage, enquiry should be made of the Scottish registrar in whose district the marriage is to take place.

Further information may be obtained from the Registrar General (see address in 26 above).

One Party Resident in Ireland

29   Where one of the parties lives in Northern Ireland or the Irish Republic and the other in England or Wales, a marriage may take place in England or Wales in a church or chapel of the Church of England or the Church in Wales after the banns or by common licence.

30   If the residence of one of the parties is in Northern Ireland a marriage may be solemnized in England or Wales in a nonconformist registered building, a register office, according to the usages of the Society of Friends or the Jews or, with the consent of the clergyman, in a church or chapel of the Church of England on the authority of a SR's certificate in respect of the party living in England or Wales and a certificate issued by a District Registrar of Marriages in Northern Ireland in respect of the party living there.

For information as to the procedure to be followed by the party resident in Northern Ireland, application should be made to the Registrar General, General Register Office, Oxford House, 49-55 Chichester Street, Belfast BT1 4HF.

31   If, however, one of the parties lives in the Irish Republic and the marriage is to take place in England or Wales notice cannot be given to a SR until that party arrives in England or Wales and has acquired the necessary residential qualification.

Marriage in Ireland

32   The party living in England or Wales may give notice to the SR of the District in which he/she has resided for the preceding seven days and obtain his certificate for production to the District Registrar in Ireland. If the marriage is to be solemnized in a church or chapel of the Church of Ireland or in accordance with the usages of the Society of Friends or the Jews, notice may be given for marriage by certificate. In the case of a marriage in a registered building or the office of a District Registrar of Marriages, notice may be given for marriage either by certificate or by certificate and licence. In any case seven days must elapse between the date on which notice is given and the date on which the SR's certificate is issued. After this has been issued a period of seven days must elapse before the certificate becomes

effective for production to the District Registrar in Ireland and if the marriage is to be solemnized without licence the ceremony cannot take place until after the expiration of 21 days after the date of entry of the notice. Notice cannot be accepted by a SR in England or Wales for a marriage in Ireland in any Roman Catholic Church or certified Presbyterian meeting house.

33 If the party giving notice in England and Wales for a marriage in the Irish Republic has not reached the age of 21 years enquiries should be made of the registrar in the Irish Republic to ascertain what evidence of consent to the marriage it will be necessary to produce.

Further information about marriage in Northern Ireland may be obtained from the Registrar General, General Register Office (see address in 30 above). For marriage in the Irish Republic from the Registrar General, Joyce House, 8-11 Lombard Street East, Dublin 2.

Marriage of Persons Domiciled outside England and Wales

34 If either of the parties to a marriage in England or Wales has a foreign domicile,

the marriage, if performed in accordance with the requirements of English law, although valid throughout the British Commonwealth (subject to the reservations in regard to any part of the Commonwealth where there may be particular requirements, e.g. Cyprus), may not be valid in any other country unless the legal requirements of the country or countries of domicile are also complied with. The parties to the proposed marriage should, therefore, take steps to obtain satisfactory assurance upon this point by reference to the nearest Consul or other representative of the foreign state in this country. No Registration Office in England or Wales can accept responsibility with regard to such legal requirements.

35   Foreigners wishing to be married in England or Wales are warned against Marriage Agents and Interpreters who claim that they are able to procure marriages quickly without the necessary statutory residence indicated above. Any person making a false statement as to residence or any other particular contained in a notice of marriage is liable to prosecution for perjury.

CIVIL
CEREMONY

Although technically the marriage must take 'place with open doors', a register office cannot accommodate too many guests. It cannot offer the atmosphere, the traditions, the symbolism and age-old rituals that a religious ceremony offers. Nevertheless, some couples deliberately choose a register office to be free of any religious obligations. It may be that they hold different religious beliefs or they may have been divorced.

A civil ceremony entails no religious service. Vows are exchanged before a Superintendent Registrar and two witnesses - usually the best man and the bride's father but they can be complete strangers. The marriage register is signed by each of the newly-weds and the two witnesses.

As is the case with church ceremonies, it is common practice for the groom to place the wedding ring on the bride's finger but this has no legal significance under civil law.

A Superintendent Registrar is duty bound to perform a marriage ceremony for divorced persons so long as the decree absolute has been granted and all other legal requirements have been met. There is no limit to the number of marriages which can be contracted by any individual (in the UK) provided that their former partner is dead or that their decree absolute is granted in the case of divorce. Some ministers may be prepared to remarry divorcees and those who refuse, may be prepared to offer a church service of blessing following the civil ceremony.

The civil ceremony takes approximately 10 minutes and the wedding party should arrive 10 minutes before ceremony time. Being earlier may cause confusion with earlier parties. Register offices may be booked well in advance for Saturdays and other popular times but they do not take bookings more than 3 months in advance.

The Registrar will advise on the ceremony procedure, number of guests allowed, flowers, music and confetti. Brides often wear best dresses or early cocktail attire and carry a small bouquet. Veils are unnecessary; a hat may be more appropriate. There are no bridesmaids or page boys.

DOUBLE AND TRIPLE WEDDINGS

Double weddings are not uncommon but ceremonies involving the simultaneous marriage of three couples are rare. There is no restriction on mass weddings linking together any number of couples at the same time.

CHURCH
WEDDING

It is traditional for weddings to take place in the bride's parish church. The tradition of banns was introduced in the 14th century by the Archbishop of Canterbury whereby the public are invited to come forward if they know of a just cause or impediment why a couple should not be married. At one time it was thought unlucky for the bride and groom to hear the reading of the banns, but today it is expected that they will attend church.

The minister should be approached as soon as possible and a wedding date organised well in advance. Waiting lists are common at certain times of the year. Services may also have to be held during certain hours and legally doors must remain open. The minister will ask to see the couple nearer to the wedding date to explain the meaning of the vows that will be made. He will instruct about procedures, including the publishing of banns.

ANNOUNCEMENT

The minister will advise on a parish magazine entry.

GIVER-AWAY

The giver-away is usually the father of the bride, but it is acceptable for others to perform this

function, such as the bride's mother.
Alternatively, it is not necessary to have the
'giving-away' ceremony in the service at all.

VOWS

Two options:

- Repeat short phrases after the minister;
- Learn phrases by rote and perhaps stand
  facing each other so that family and friends
  can see and hear more.

SERVICE

Three options:

- Book of Common Prayer 1662; Most ancient
  includes promise of obedience to husband
- Book of Common Prayer 1928; Excludes
  promise of obedience.
- Alternative Service 1980; Leaves obedience
  to the couple and offers a selection of prayers.

MUSIC

The role of music is to:

- Fill in time before arrival;
- Set the scene;
- Herald the arrival of the bride;
- Accompany the walk down the aisle;
- Occupy and interest the congregation during

the signing of the register.
• Enable the congregation to take an active part.

The minister should be asked for his views. He may insist that it be religious, or allow something more secular. However, a rock band may not be a good idea. Consider the length of the music when choosing the piece to coincide with the walk down the aisle.

Organ
Popular Wedding Music:

Entrance of the Bride

A Wedding Fanfare	Bliss
Arrival of the Queen of Sheba	Handel
Wedding March from the marriage of Figaro	Mozart
Fanfare	Purcell

Signing of the Register

Air on the G String	Bach
Ave Maria	Bach
Jesu, Joy of Man's Desiring	Bach
Benediction Nuptiale	Saint-Saens

Exit of Bride and Groom

Pomp and Circumstance March No. 4	Elgar
Bridal March	Hollins
Wedding March from A Midsummer Night's Dream	Mendelssohn
Wedding March from Lohengrin	Wagner

Music played at weddings is considered 'private' and is exempt from copyright fees.

Hymns

There are usually three:

- On arrival when standing before the chancel steps;
- After the marriage ceremony;
- After the blessing.

Choir and Bell-ringers

If there is a choir, it is advisable to ensure that it is strong enough to sing the chosen hymns. If there is no choir, it is advisable to select popular hymns.

Choir members and bell-ringers tend to disband in August.

Many churches do not permit bell-ringing during church festivals such as Lent (between Shrove Tuesday and Easter) and Advent (about a month before Christmas). So if you are hoping to hear wedding bells, you had better check with the minister.

Singers and Relatives Reading the Lessons

The minister may be consulted with any special requests.

Taping the Ceremony
The minister must give permission.

FLOWERS
Many churches do not permit flowers to decorate the church during church festivals such as Lent (between Shrove Tuesday and Easter) and Advent (about a month before Christmas).

CONFETTI
If allowed, there may be a charge and if not, there could be acceptable alternatives, e.g. rice, wild bird food, fresh flower petals. It is important that the minister's instructions are followed.

Local litter laws should be checked. If the church door opens directly on to the street, confetti will not be allowed.

COLLECTION
There may be a stipulation that a collection is taken.

PHOTOGRAPHS AND VIDEO
Photographs may be allowed if flash is not used, but there may be restrictions in the vestry. The minister's instructions must be followed.

The minister must also be consulted regarding video recording.

REHEARSAL

The date and time of the rehearsal should be agreed with the minister.

CHARGES

- Banns ⎱ Fixed by
- Certificate ⎰ Church Commissioners
- Verger
- Organist ⎱ Fixed by
- Choir the minister
- Bell-ringers ⎰

It is advisable to pay church fees in advance rather than entrust the best man to do this immediately after the ceremony.

Since the minister puts in so much effort for which he receives no direct payment, it may be appropriate to consider a personal donation to his church. He may stipulate that a collection should be made at the end of the service.

HELP SOURCES

EXHIBITIONS, SHOWS AND FAIRS

Details of bridal exhibitions, shows and fairs featuring all wedding requirements, e.g. gowns, suit hire, cakes, flowers, videos, photographs, discos, headdress, hair, wines, travel, lingerie, shoes, crystal, cars, etc. can be found in the local press.

PUBLICATIONS

Magazines are published at various intervals and can be obtained from newsagents. Some current publications are listed on the next page.
Further listings appear in Willings Press Guide and BRAD (published by Maclean Hunter) available from the reference section of local libraries.

Publication	**Frequency**	**Publisher**
Bride & Groom First Home	Alternate months	Casper Publishers, Dublin
Brides Setting Up Home	Alternate months	The Condé Nast Publications, London
Brides of (various yearly	Twice Britain	Brides of places) Magazine, Berkshire
Wedding Book	Annual	Home & Law Publishing
Wedding & Home Consumer	Alternate	Maxwell months Publications, London
Weddings & Special Occasions	Annual	Butterick Co, Hampshire
You & Your Wedding	Thrice yearly	AIM Publications

FINANCE

RESPONSIBILITY FOR PAYMENT

Tradition
Traditionally the burden has fallen heavily on the bride's father, who inherits the dowry tradition: the groom confers an honour on the bride's family by marrying her, and he has to be rewarded.

In the past fathers have been expected to pay for:

Bride's clothes (wedding and going-away attire);

Bridesmaids' dresses (today, the cost may be shared with the groom's parents and/or the bridesmaids' mothers);

Beauty treatments;

Press announcements;

Stationery;

Transport to the ceremony;

Photographs/video;

Flowers for church and reception;

Reception (today, increasingly, the groom's parents contribute or even undertake the whole cost);

Cake.

The groom's family would pay for:

Groom's clothes (wedding and going-away attire);
Ushers' clothes;
Bride's wedding ring;
Church fees (excluding flowers);
Flowers for the bride (including bouquet);
Bridesmaids' (and mothers') bouquets;
Bridesmaids' gifts;
Buttonholes;
Transport for bride and groom after the ceremony;
Honeymoon;
Petty cash for best man.

There are now very few families who adhere to tradition as this does not reflect equality.

FINANCIAL ARRANGEMENTS

Estimates
Beware, estimates give only a general idea of final cost, and may be quite inaccurate, not exposing hidden extras.

Quotations
A quotation is usually a fixed price for a specified job. It is advisable to obtain

quotations, check delivery charges and the possibility of price increases.

Methods of Payment

It is reasonable for a supplier to want advance payment to confirm authenticity. The deposit may be non-returnable in the case of cancellation or it may be part-payment of the final bill.

Methods of payment should be agreed in advance.

Contracts for Goods and Services

Small print of which to be aware: 'subject to price fluctuation' and 'price payable shall be that prevailing at delivery time'.

BUDGET

A budget should be fixed with a contingency fund included from the outset. A comprehensive list may then be produced.

Item	Estimate	Quotation		Actual	
		Deposit Paid		Bal Due	Date Due
£	£	£		£	

Bride's Budget List

Clothes:	Bride	-	Dress
		-	Train
		-	Veil/headdress/hat
		-	Shoes
		-	Underclothes
		-	Garter
		-	Hosiery
		-	Something old, something new, something borrowed something blue!
		-	Going-away outfit
	Bridesmaids	-	Dresses
		-	
Beauty		-	Hair
		-	Make-up
		-	
		-	
Press		-	
Stationery		-	Invitations
		-	Map
		-	Order of service sheets
		-	Menus
		-	Place name cards
		-	Cake boxes and liners
		-	Bridal notepaper
		-	Diary
Transport to the ceremony		-	
Photographs/video		-	
Flowers		-	Church
		-	Reception
Reception		-	
		-	
		-	Cake
Ring			

Groom's Budget List

Clothes	Groom	-	Suit
		-	Shirt
		-	Tie
		-	Going-away outfit
		-	
		-	
	Ushers	-	
		-	
Church fees		-	Banns
		-	Certificate
		-	Verger
		-	Organist
		-	Choir
		-	Bell-ringers
		-	
		-	
Flowers	Bride	-	Bouquet
		-	
	Bridesmaids	-	
		-	
	Mothers	-	
		-	
	Buttonholes	-	
		-	
		-	
Ring		-	
Gifts	Bridesmaids	-	
Transport	Bride and groom after ceremony	-	
Honeymoon		-	
Petty cash	Best man	-	

RECEPTION

The purpose of a reception after the wedding ceremony is to:

Allow wedding guests to congratulate the newly-weds;

Join in toasts to the health and happiness of the couple;

Witness the cutting of the cake;

Wish The couple well as they leave for honeymoon;

Provide an opportunity for the two families to communicate.

VENUE OPTIONS

Hotel

Advantages	*Disadvantages*
Organised food, drink, cake	Possibly the most expensive
Less work	Possibly impersonal
Delegation of responsibility	Numbers may be limited
	Mass-produced production line
Predictable cost	Need for advance booking
Range of prices	Times may be restricted,
Range of menus	particularly on Saturdays
General comfort	(perhaps a rival
Car parking	function!)
Overnight accommodation	VAT payable
Dance/disco option	

Halls, eg Village/School/Church

Advantages
Accommodation of large
   numbers
Choice of sit-down meal
   or buffet
Freedom
Car parking
Inexpensive
Disco/dance possible

Disadvantages
Often bare and functional
Limited catering facilities,
   e.g. cooker, fridge
Shortage of electric points
Doubtful heating
Shortage/non-existence of
   gas supply
Inadequate water supply
Insufficient chairs
Need to hire equipment
Problem of matching caterers
   with facilities
Cleanliness must be checked
   the day prior
Inadequate toilet facilities -
   soap, towels, coat hangers
Poor cloakroom facilities
Cleaning up/refuse disposal
   arrangements
Inadequate washing-up
   facilities
No licence for alcohol
Time restrictions
Decoration of hall
Smoking may invalidate
   insurance cover
Insufficient chairs, tables,
   crockery

Home

Advantages	Disadvantages
Personal, intimate, friendly	Numbers generally limited
	Tendency to crowd
Freedom	Hard work
Timing is flexible	Requires organisation in Cheap
unpaid labour	great detail
	Clearing up
	Inadequate cloakroom and toilet facilities
	Hire/borrow: chairs, tables, china, cutlery and glasses
	Hire wine waiter
	Organise wine
	No one to blame if things go wrong!

Marquee/Garden Party

Advantages	Disadvantages
Freedom	Weather!
Timing is flexible	Insufficient space
	Outside caterers
	Access to/from house
facilities - hire	Insufficient cloakroom/ toilet portaloo
	Inadequate car parking
	Music may be impossible
	Expensive
	Labour intensive
	Need for awnings, flooring and partitions.

Venues With Catering Provided

After considering several options you might like to try the venues yourself, to check the standard of the food produced.

As soon as the venue is selected, a firm booking should be made and written confirmation obtained. Most hotels can only deal with one or two weddings per day and they may be booked up well in advance, some 2 to 3 years.

Checklist

Date
Time
Number of guests
Menus
       - special dietary requirements
Wine   - if supplied separately, a corkage charge may
          apply
       - sale or return basis
Soft drinks
Seating arrangements
Speeches   - timing
Cake   - maker
       - delivery
       - silver cake stand and knife with white satin
          ribbon
Flowers   - provider/supplier
       - type
       - entrance hall and central displays
       - tables (posies perhaps)
Napkins
Candles

Bride's changing room
Accommodation   - overnight
Cloakroom and toilet facilities   - adequacy
                                    - duty person
Extension   - licence if late disco/
                                       dance
Car park
Insurance cover   - liability and gifts
Service charge
Tips
Overall cost (so that a cost per person may be calculated)
VAT   - included/excluded
Deposit/cancellation fee
Stages of payments

Outside Caterer

A firm of caterers will suggest suitable menus, provide linen, china and silver, serve food and drinks and clear up.

    Standards and prices vary enormously. It is advisable to select from personal recommendation or from experience.

Checklist
Qualifications
Experience   - references
Capability   - ability to cope with number of guests
Date agreement

Meal options	- sit-down	: hot
	- sit-down	: cold (fork buffet)
	- stand	: finger buffet

Set dishes
Options
Special dietary requirements

| Wines | - servers |
| | - if supplied separately, there may be a |

corkage charge

| | - if caterer supplies, sale-or-return |
| | basis? |

Serving the guests
Cake cutting
Food preparation location
Cutlery, crockery, glassware, cake-stand, table cloths
Number of trestle tables for exhibition of wedding gifts

| Table arrangements | - flowers, napkins, candles |

Seating arrangements
Terms for damage/breakages

| Inspection | - caterers will wish to see the facilities |

Insurance
Cost
Deposit/cancellation fee

| Payment | - in advance |
| | - in stages |

VAT
Service charge
Tips

Self-Catering

Self-catering demands considerable and total commitment. Ample time and appropriate temperament are essential. There needs to be total certainty that this is the right choice. Capabilities and facilities must not be over-estimated. It is advisable not to be too ambitious, to keep things simple and to accept offers of help.

Options	
Number of guests	*Function*
6-8	Small dinner party
30	Buffet
50	Hire of hall

Checklist

Menu	- plan to suit facilities available
	- special dietary requirements
	- if there are menu choices, inform guests by displaying menu cards at table
Space	- consider space available for preparation, cooking, storage, service and clearing up
Timing	
Equipment	- list
Rally the troops	
Allocate jobs	
Appoint	- close, competent friend(s) to be organiser(s) on the day
	- drinks allocator
Records	- keep written notes as to who does what
Accounts	- ensure prompt payment to those buying items on behalf of organiser

Instructions   - issue jobs lists
Schedule   - draw up timetable
Quantities   - calculate carefully and allow for
                                    stock of reserves in case of
                                    emergency
Prepare as much as possible in advance
Carriage   - consider carriage to venue
Transport   - to venue
Flowers
Napkins
Candles
Towels, toilet rolls, soap
Ashtrays
Valuables and breakables out of sight
Stationery, eg menu cards
Buffet line up:
Cutlery - Bread - Dessert - Vegetables - Salads - Meat - Plates
Condiments (work from right to left)
Waiters/waitresses   - can be hired.
                                1:20 is a reasonable ratio of skilled
                                    staff to guests
                                - uniform/dress change
                                    arrangements
                                - refreshment facilities
                                - tip them before reception

CAKE

The cake has pride of place at the reception. The first slice is cut ceremonially by the bride and groom. It is then removed and cut professionally behind the scenes. Small slices are handed round on paper napkins so that they may be taken away by anyone not wishing to eat the cake at that time.

The cake must be ordered many weeks in advance of the wedding; ideally the cake should stand for six to nine weeks before it is iced.

Types
Classic rich fruit cake
Biscuit wheat sheaf
White frosted Swiss roll stuffed with glacé
    cherries
French pyramid of profriteroles

Style and Shape
Often the cake is tiered with cakes of diminishing size one on top of the other. The bottom (largest) cake is cut and a top layer may be kept for future use, say at a christening. Cake that is to be kept should be wrapped in tissue paper and placed in an airtight tin. The fruit will gradually seep through, discolouring the icing, but the cake can be re-iced when necessary.

Tiered cake	pillared	- round cake with round pillars
		- square cake with square pillars
	stacked	- with tiers sitting directly on top of each other

Size

Volume	- consider the number of guests
Height	- consider the height of the cake depending on your own height, and where it will be placed at the reception
Colour	- the cake can be any colour to match wedding decor, but traditionally is white

DRINK

It is becoming increasingly popular to serve sparking wines throughout the reception, or a still white wine with a good champagne for the toasts.

If a combination of wine is to be served, the order is: dry white, red, younger, older.

In addition to the above, there should always be a plentiful supply of fresh fruit juices and soft drinks.

You may also consider serving sherry as guests arrive at the reception, include a dry fino, a medium amontillado and a sweet oloroso.

As an accompaniment to meals, the tradition of white wine with fish and red wine with most meats is no longer strictly adhered to. Usually two out of three people prefer white wine. An expert should be consulted for detailed information.

Champagnes, white wines and sherries should be adequately chilled. Ideal bottle temperature is 42-48° F (5.5-9° C) but two to three hours in cold water will suffice where no ice is available.

Red wines should be served at room temperature (two hours in the dining-room should suffice) and uncorked one hour prior to being served to allow for breathing.

Champagne is the traditional wedding drink but can be very expensive. A half to three quarters of a bottle per person should be allowed if champagne is to be served throughout the reception. A bottle will serve six glasses, and will therefore be sufficient for six people if just used for the toasts.

In the case of wine, half a 75cl bottle should be allowed for each guest.

SEATING PLAN

A table plan should be displayed near to the entrance of the dining-room so that guests will be able to go directly to their places where place cards confirm their positions.

Top Table

The main bridal party sits along one side of a table facing the guests, thus ensuring that everyone can view the top table.

Suggested seating plans.

Best man	Groom's father	Bride's mother	G B	Bride's father	Groom's mother	Chief brides-maid

xxxxxxxxxxxxxxxxxxxxxxxxxxxxxxxxxxxxxxxxxxxxxxxxxxxx

Bridesmaids		x			Bridesmaids
x		x			x
Ushers		x			Ushers

Or as above but swop the chief bridesmaid with the best man.

Groom's mother	Bride's father	Chief brides-maid	G B	Best man	Bride's mother	Groom's father

Chief brides-maid	Bride's father	Bride's mother	G B	Groom's father	Groom's mother	Best man

---

Other Tables

Brothers and sisters should be interspersed with their wives and husbands as applicable. Aunts and uncles follow and then friends of the newly-weds.

An attempt should be made to alternate the sexes as far as possible, always considering friendships or otherwise.

The bride's family and friends could occupy the tables on the groom's side and vice versa or families could be mixed.

Suggested layouts

Ideal-Everybody has a clear view of everybody else

HONEYMOON

Traditionally the honeymoon is taken immediately after the wedding, but increasingly the bride and groom prefer a holiday some time afterwards when all the activity has subsided. If the groom-to-be arranges a surprise venue, it is advisable and courteous to give the bride-to-be some indication of the climate so that she may plan attire accordingly. It is a good idea to have a change from what will be, for the future, normal routine.

Passports and medical requirements must be finalised well in advance. Arrangements for pets must also be made.

ROLES

The allocation of roles is more a matter of custom and tradition than the demands of either ecclesiastical or secular law.

BRIDESMAIDS

These are unmarried attendants.

A widow remarrying would not be supported by bridesmaids but by a 'dame of honour' whose only duty is to wait at the chancel steps to relieve the bride of her bouquet.

Young children may be cute as bridesmaids, but can be a nuisance.

Duties

Help with the bride's dress before and after the ceremony;

Get into car (destined for ceremony) leaving the bride alone with mother and giver-away for a few minutes;

Look after wedding clothes;

Carry comb and pocket mirror for use by the bride;

Hand out slices of cake.

CHIEF BRIDESMAID

The chief bridesmaid is usually the eldest unmarried sister or another unmarried relative or friend.

Duties
Helps the bride to choose bridesmaids' dresses;
Marshalls the bridesmaids and pages;
Takes charge of the bride's bouquet during the
service;
Helps bride to dress in her going-away outfit.

Tradition
*Traditionally, when the bridal couple return from
honeymoon, the chief bridesmaid would wait
at their home and welcome them.
This tradition is now often carried out by the bride's
mother and / or her mother-in-law.*

MATRON OF HONOUR
The matron of honour is a married lady
attendant, sometimes chosen instead of
bridesmaids when she will be the only attendant
acting as chief and only bridesmaid.

Duties
Her duties are the same as those of a chief
bridesmaid but she will not wear the finery.

BEST MAN
The 'best person' can be a woman but as duties
include helping the groom to dress, it would be
more usual to have a best man.

The best person is generally chosen by the groom. Traditionally best men were bachelors but today, married men are acceptable.

Duties

Compiles a list of close family and hands this to the ushers to help them with seating arrangements at the church;

Liaises with ushers beforehand;

Prevents the organisation of the stag party for the eve of the wedding;

Arranges transport for groom and himself and going away vehicle for newly-weds;

Collects buttonholes for groom and himself;

Checks arrangements, ushers, buttonholes and order of service sheets;

Checks parking arrangements and transport between service and reception;

Oversees and supervises ushers;

Holds extra name card blanks in case of the arrival of unexpected guests at the reception;

Holds a list of alternative photographers in case the appointed photographer fails to show;

Holds spare order of service sheets for unexpected friends at church;

Holds and safeguards ring(s);

Acts as baggage master;

Ensures that the groom's going-away clothes are ready at reception;

Helps groom to dress;

Superstition

The best man ensures good luck for the couple by ensuring that the groom carries a small mascot in his pocket.

Accompanies the groom to the church, ensuring that he is there on time;

Superstition

The best man should ensure good luck for the couple by not allowing the groom to turn back for any reason after starting out for the ceremony.

Takes charge of groom's hat and gloves in church Accompanies chief bridesmaid to vestry behind the bride and groom;
Signs register (if called upon to do so);
Pays church fees to the minister;

Superstition

The best man ensures the good luck of the couple by giving an odd sum of money to the minister for his fee.

Follows bride and groom out of the church with bridesmaids;
Escorts newly-weds to the photographer once outside the church;

Escorts bride and groom to their car;

Escorts guests into their cars in order: parents, grandparents, uncles and aunts, bridesmaids, other relatives, friends;

Supervises reception, ensuring that guests are correctly seated;

Decides when cake should be cut and when bride and groom should change;

Calls for speakers at the reception;

Replies on behalf of the bridesmaids in response to a toast to their health;

Reads messages;

Sees newly-weds to their car after reception;

Returns groom's wedding clothes;

Ensures that nothing is left behind at the reception;

Carries petty-cash in case of emergency and ensures that everyone is paid (the groom reimburses expenses upon return from honeymoon);

Deals with transport arrangements;

Holds documentation, e.g. tickets, passports;

Ensures that couple's luggage is correctly labelled and is ready for transportation;

Together with chief bridesmaid, checks that all gifts are carefully stored and that clothes have been taken away and returned to the hire company (if appropriate).

USHERS

These should include family members; one from each side, usually unmarried brothers or close friends. They are chosen by the groom in consultation with the best man.

Duties

Receive list of close family from best man to help with seating arrangements;

Liaise with best man beforehand;

Have a single red carnation instead of a single white one;

Arrive first at the church;

Allocate buttonholes;

Hand out hymn books, prayer books and/or order of service sheets;

Show guests to seats at church and reception, guiding any unescorted lady to her seat;

Ensure that the church is left tidy, e.g. collection of service sheets;

Clean up confetti (if appropriate).

PAGES

These are usually very young (5 to 8 years of age).

BRIDE'S MOTHER

Duties

Acts as hostess;

Arranges press announcements;

Organises stationery;

Organises church decorations;

Organises bouquets and buttonholes and perhaps corsages for the two mothers;

Orders wedding cars to transport bride and giver-away, bridesmaids and herself, and other guests to the service. (The transport for the groom and best man is not her responsibility);

Arranges delivery of wedding cake to reception;

Arranges for a photographer;

Decides and arranges reception: menu, wines, table décor, table and seating plan, books private room for bride;

Arranges overnight accommodation for guests;

Helps the bride to dress;

Ensures that there is a seat beside her for the giver-away who will join her after he has fulfilled his duty;

Led by groom's father to vestry to witness the signing of the register;

Leaves the church on the left arm of the groom's father following bridesmaids and pages in procession with the groom's mother and bride's father behind them;

Leaves the church with the giver-away immediately after the newly-weds to host reception;

Takes charge of cake after reception;

Sends slices of cake to those who were unable to attend the wedding.

GIVER-AWAY

He is usually the bride's father, but if dead or physically incapable, the bride's eldest brother or male guardian or uncle may take on the role.

Duties

Wears buttonhole similar to that worn by groom and best man;

Escorts bride from her home to church;

Leads procession to chancel steps with bride on his right arm;

Gives away the bride;

Accompanies groom's mother to vestry after the service;

Arrives first at the reception with bride's mother to host reception;

Proposes toast of the bride and groom if called upon to do so by best man;

Pays for reception.

BRIDE

Duties

Discusses payment;

Decides on church or register office;

Selects and appoints chief bridesmaid, bridesmaids and pages;

Chooses helpers in agreement with her fiancè;

Chooses attire for attendants (as above);

Acquires own gown and going-away outfit;

Acquires luggage;

Chooses stationery;

Arranges press announcements (with mother);

Books photographer (with mother);

Compiles guest list;

Orders cake;

Orders flowers, bouquets, buttonholes and corsages;

Orders wedding cars to church and reception;

Arranges service: date, order of service, music, church decorations;

Decides and organises reception: venue, date, menu and wines;

Arranges for display of wedding gifts.

GROOM

Duties

Selects best man and ushers;

Chooses helpers in agreement with his fiancèe;

Arranges stag party;

Purchases or hires own outfit;

Purchases ring(s);

Arranges honeymoon: booking, passports, traveller's cheques, inoculations (if necessary);

Arranges transport from reception, in consultation with best man.

GUEST LIST

Resentments can linger and affect relationships, so it should be remembered that consultation and compromise are essential. If young children are excluded, this may also exclude their parents if they are unable to arrange baby-sitters. On the other hand, can a bawling infant or an insuppressible toddler be tolerated for a whole day? Letters of explanation (rejection) must be extremely tactful - even the nearest and dearest are sensitive about their children.

Traditionally the bride's mother compiles the guest list in consultation with the groom's family. Today it largely depends on the payer of the bill. Whoever is giving the reception must be firm and decide on a maximum number. The uninvited may still attend church or registry office and may also send gifts.

STATIONERY

INVITATIONS

It is the duty of the bride's family to despatch invitations, but the guest list should be a compendium of suggestions from both the bride's and the groom's sides. Invitations are usually from and sent by the bride's parents, indicating their responsibility for the payment of the reception. An invitation is sent to the groom's parents.

Invitations should be despatched simultaneously as no prospective guest likes to assume that he or she is a second choice. Invitations should be despatched at least six weeks prior to the wedding.

The name and full address of the place of marriage should be checked for accuracy as in some towns there may be several churches all dedicated to the same saint.

The names of the guests are formally handwritten in the top left-hand corner, e.g.

Mr and Mrs Gerald Green

If a child is included:

Mr and Mrs Gerald Green and Joe

If there is to be a disco or dance after the

reception, this should be stated with an indication of suitable dress, in the bottom right-hand corner of the invitation.

Typical Wording

Wedding given by Bride's Parents

Mr and Mrs Nigel North
request the pleasure of your company/
request the company of ...
at the marriage of their daughter
Nel
to Mr Samuel South
at St Mark's Church, Northton
on Saturday 2 May 19 .. at 2.30 p.m.
and afterwards at Stone Manor, Northton

3 Rose Lane
Northton NT1 2AB   RSVP

Wedding given by Bride and Groom

Nel North and Samuel South
request the pleasure of your company/
request the company of ...
at their marriage
at ...

Wedding given jointly by Parents of Bride and Groom

Mr and Mrs Nigel North
and
Mr and Mrs Sidney South
request the pleasure of your company/
request the company of ...
at the marriage of
Nel
to
Samuel South
at ...

Wedding given by Bride's Divorced Mother (now Re-married and her Husband)

Mr and Mrs Benjamin Black
request the pleasure of your company/
request the company of ...
at the marriage of her daughter
Nel North
to
Samuel South
at ...

Wedding given by Bride's Divorced Mother (now Re-married) and Bride's Father

Mr Nigel North and Mrs Nancy Black
request the pleasure of your company/
request the company of ...
at the marriage of their daughter

...

Bride's Divorced Father (now Re-married) and his Wife

Mr and Mrs Nigel North
request the pleasure of your company at the marriage of
his daughter
Nel North
to
Mr Samuel South
at ...

Wedding given by Widowed Mother who has not Re-married

Mrs Nancy North
requests the pleasure ...

Wedding given by Widowed Mother who has since Re-married

Mr and Mrs Benjamin Black
request the pleasure ...
at the marriage of her/their daughter

Wedding given by Widowed Father who has not Re-married

Mr Nigel North
requests the pleasure ...

Wedding given by Others, e.g. if Bride's Parents are Deceased

Mr and Mrs Guy Grey
request the pleasure of your company at the marriage
of
Nel North
daughter of the late Mr and Mrs Nigel North
to
Mr Samuel South

Civil Ceremony - Invitation to Reception

Mr and Mrs Nigel North
request the pleasure of your company
following the marriage of their daughter
Nel North
to Mr Samuel South
on ...
at ...

Service of Blessing

Mr and Mrs Nigel North
request the pleasure of your company
at a Service of Blessing following the marriage of their
daughter
Nel North
to Mr Samuel South
at ...
on ...
and afterwards at ...

Reception Only Invitations

Mr and Mrs Nigel North
request the pleasure of/
request the company of ...
at the Reception
to celebrate the marriage of their daughter
Nel North
to Samuel South
to be held at
Stone Manor, Northton
on Saturday 2 May 19 ..
at 4.30 pm

3 Rose Lane
Northton NT1 2AB   RSVP

Evening Only Invitations

Mr and Mrs Nigel North request the pleasure of/
request the company of ...
on the evening of the wedding of their daughter
Nel
to
Mr Samuel South
at Stone Manor, Northton
on Saturday 2 May 19 ..
at 8.00 pm

Mr and Mrs Nigel North
request the pleasure of/

...

at an evening reception at ...
to celebrate the marriage
of their daughter

...

to

...

on ...

Address   RSVP

Map

It is a good idea to photocopy a map and
highlight relevant places, e.g. church, reception
venue, railway station, taxi ranks, bus stops, car
parking. If cars are to be provided, the statement
needs to be clear, 'Cars will meet trains ...'.

REPLIES TO INVITATIONS

Acceptance

Guests should reply formally, briefly and promptly.

> Date   Address
> Mr and Mrs Gerald Green and their son accept with pleasure Mr and Mrs North's kind invitation to the marriage of their daughter, Nel, to Mr Samuel South at St Mark's Church, Northton on ... at ... and afterwards at ...
> (No signature required)

Early Refusal

It is courteous to acknowledge the invitation and to state apologies clearly. The refusal should be formal, brief and sent promptly.

> Date   Address
> Mr and Mrs Gerald Green and their son thank Mr and Mrs North for their kind invitation to their daughter's wedding at ... on ... and to the reception afterwards. Unfortunately, they have accepted a prior engagement for that particular date and must therefore decline with regret.
> (No signature required)

Late Refusal

Unforeseen circumstances may necessitate a late refusal following acceptance. A note should be sent immediately.

> Date   Address
> Mr and Mrs Gerald Green and their son sincerely regret the necessity, because of a bereavement in the family, to have to inform you that they will now be unable to attend your daughter's wedding on ... or the reception afterwards.
> (No signature required)

ORDER OF SERVICE SHEETS

These provide a guide to the service and include the words of hymns but they can be an unnecessary expense where a sufficient number of hymn books are provided.

When calculating how many sheets to order, remember to include the minister, attendants and choir, as well as the guests. Order a few extra for unexpected friends.

The groom holds two copies and passes one to the bride. Bridesmaids acquire their copies from pew ends when they reach the chancel steps.

MENUS

If a formal meal is being served, menus may be considered. However, they are an optional extra and, obviously, incur additional expense.

PLACE NAME CARDS

Full names should be used. In the case of a divorced or separated lady, her own initials of her first name should be used. The best man should hold additional blanks in case of the arrival of unexpected guests.

COMPLIMENTS CARDS AND CAKE BOXES

Compliments cards are despatched with pieces of cake to those unable to attend on the day.

Mr and Mrs Samuel South
(address)
With compliments on the occasion of their wedding
2 May 19 ..

OTHER IDEAS FOR THE RECEPTION

Some couples like to have personalised printed matter for the reception, including monogrammed napkins or napkin rings, drink mats and match boxes.

BRIDAL NOTEPAPER

Special paper showing the couple's new address and date of wedding for thank-you letters can be very useful.

PHOTOGRAPHS
AND VIDEO

• •

PHOTOGRAPHS

Perhaps the most difficult choice is the photographer. Taking good photographs requires years of experience and the professional photographer will know how best to tackle bad weather. His skill provides the most important memento of all. If a professional is employed, guests should be instructed not to take photographs. If two flash guns are fired simultaneously, then the paid-for photographs could be ruined.

It is important to check that the photographer is a full-time professional. If a photographer is a member of a professional association, he is compelled to conform to a code of practice and if it is felt that performance is unprofessional, reference can be made to the appropriate association. It is advisable to note the association(s) when visiting the photographer and to ascertain who will be taking the photographs.

A check on qualifications and the date qualified is also a good idea. Professional bodies include the Master Photographers' Association and the British Institute of Professional Photographers. Experience can be checked by examining previous work.

It would be worthwhile checking the length of

time the business has been established.

In case of illness there should be provision for a back-up photographer. It is advisable to compile a list of alternative photographers (locally based) and to ensure that the best man has this with him on the day. If the appointed photographer fails to show on the day, it may be necessary to recruit someone else at short notice.

It should be borne in mind that cheapest is not always best and that after the wedding, the photographs are all that remain of the great day.

Photography Agenda

At home

      Bride looking into her mirror;
      Father of bride greeting her when she comes downstairs.

At the ceremony
  Arrival of: Groom and best man;
      Bridesmaids and bride's mother;
      Bride and giver-away.

During the ceremony
  In the: Church;
      Vestry for signing of the register.

After the ceremony
      Leaving the church;
      Couple getting into the car.

Formal after-ceremony photographs
   (Photographer must be informed of exact location)
                      Receiving guests;
                      Cutting of the cake;
                      Proposing toast.
Leaving for the honeymoon

Choice of Photographs

Photographs may be black and white, or colour, or a mixture. The finish may be matt or gloss.

Special effects, e.g. superimposed, 'misties', or unusual backgrounds should be discussed with the photographer beforehand.

The photographs may be presented in a professional album, and could include studio portraits (taken some time before the wedding).

Charges and Advice

Some photographers charge an attendance fee which is added to the cost of the number of photographs and the album. Some also may require a deposit when the booking is made.

It is worth bearing in mind the following:

- Quotations should be obtained.
- Set number of pictures?
- Price for each finished photograph?
- Are you at liberty to keep the proofs?

- Are proofs over-stamped and therefore rendered worthless?
- Who owns copyright and negatives?
- When do prices increase?
- Check on deposit/cancellation arrangements.

VIDEO

For high-class production of a commercial standard, the services of a professional should be sought.

It is advisable to view some of his previous work before making a firm booking. Once the cameraman has been appointed, details of the couple's requirements should be discussed and agreed upon. Options include: church only; church and reception to the end of the speeches; or church, reception and full evening coverage. A visit to the bride's home to video preparations may also be included.

ATTIRE

BRIDE

Superstition
Something old, something new
Something borrowed, something blue,
And a silver sixpence/silver threepenny bit in your
shoe.

Dress and Train

It is difficult to define tradition. Brides were not
expected to wear white until the 16th century
and even then brides wore their best dresses
whatever the colour. Co-ordination is the key.
Selection of something that suits and an
awareness of the reality of figure, i.e. that which
needs hiding and that which needs highlighting,
is recommended. High prices can be paid for
originality, individuality, fabric quality and
finish but a mass-produced dress accompanied
by a personal variation of accessories will not be
instantly recognisable as such. Though the
ceremony is exactly the same where a bride
happens to be a widow, tradition calls for less
formality and suggests the omission of the bridal
gown and veil.

A groom should not see his future bride's
dress before the wedding. If she decides to wear
white, the groom should complement her by

wearing morning attire. There is no reason why a bride marrying in a register office cannot wear a white gown if she wishes. It is not, however, usual for widows or divorcees, whether remarrying in church or in a register office, to wear white.

Dress Options

Purchase	- Off the peg chain store
	- Specialist bridal wear shop
	- Specially made
Hire	- It is important to ensure prompt delivery

Figure

Stout, roundish	- Frills/flounces, puffed sleeves and any trimmings should be avoided
	- Emphasise elegant shoulders
Short	- Horizontal line, e.g. rows of frills should be avoided
Tall, thin	- Trimmings, crinoline or layers can be effective
	- Vertical stripes should be avoided
Big-busted	- High necklines should be avoided

The general principle is to create a diversion - a counter-attraction.

Old Wives' Tales

White	*You have chosen right*
Green	*You will not long be seen*
Red	*You will wish you were dead*
Yellow	*Ashamed of the fellow*
Brown	*You will live out of town*
Grey	*You will live far away*
Black	*You will wish you were back*
Pink	*Your fortunes will sink*
Blue	*Your lover is true*

Advice

- Set a budget and do not be afraid to disclose this when shopping;
- Start looking three to five months before the wedding;
- Shop around - look at shops and magazines;
- Try to avoid peak shopping times;
- Do not be bulldozed into a quick purchase;
- Retain an open mind - try on various styles, colours and lengths;
- Look at the dress in both artificial light and daylight;
- Creases should fall out instantly;
- Ensure that the dress is anti-static;
- Is it possible to breathe, walk, kneel and eat?

- Try on all accessories with the dress;
- Do not ignore the backview;
- Gloves may be appropriate;
- Plan fitting arrangements if appropriate;
- Check arrangements for alterations;
- Ensure that delivery dates and alteration times are guaranteed in writing;
- Check cancellation policies;
- Methods of payment - credit cards allow more time to pay and certain bank cards give extra legal protection;
- Check dress after purchase. Lay flat and press (very cool iron) the day before the wedding.

Veil or Head-dress or Hat

The veil did not appear until the 19th century and since then it has become very popular and is still recognised as being symbolic of the bride and her chastity. Traditionally the bride's veil is thrown back after the ceremony, revealing her face. Old lace veils are heavy to wear and are best held in place by a heavy tiara. Alice bands or circlets can be used to hold other types of veil. Silk net is expensive but light to wear and easy to hold in place. Nylon net is the least expensive but is slippery and difficult to keep in place. Popular veil lengths include shoulder, hand, floor, or even longer.

Head-dresses can be worn with or without a veil. Purchased head-dresses can look superb. Materials can include: pearls, diamanté, silk or fresh flowers (to match bride's and bridesmaids' flowers).

Strictly speaking, if a bride and attendants wear hats, they should not carry bouquets as well. A prayer-book is now quite popular.

Shoes

It would be foolish to wear very high-heeled shoes. Non-slip soles are a good idea and fabric may be dyed to achieve the correct colour. Shoes (old or new) should be tried on with the dress when shopping for it. It is worth practising walking about to ensure comfort and non-rub and slip. Remember to remove the price sticker from the base.

Underclothes

Try these on with the dress. Ensure that the bra cannot be seen through the dress and that the straps are not visible.

Tradition
Wearing a garter is believed to bring good luck.

Tights or stockings? The best advice is to wear the usual. If the dress is white, ultra-pale hosiery looks good.

Going-away Outfit
This can be anything the bride-to-be fancies.

GROOM

Options

Morning Suit, Top Hat and Gloves (usually carried)
Formal attire should complement the bride in white. A black or grey swallow tail coat, striped trousers and grey silk hat is the traditional attire. (The hat is removed on entering the church and is carried by the brim together with the gloves in the left hand, leaving the right one free for shaking hands. When the groom approaches the chancel steps, he leaves his hat and gloves in the pew.)

Lounge Suit (dark colour)
Less formal and very popular. No hat is worn. The shirt should be white and tie pale blue or grey with little or no pattern.

A lounge suit would be appropriate for the marriage of a widower.

Dinner Jacket
This should be worn with a dark tie.

Evening Wear
This is the groom's personal choice.

BEST MAN, FATHERS OF THE BRIDE AND GROOM, USHERS

Regardless of what other men wear, traditionally the above follow the groom's lead. If he wears formal attire, then so should they.

MATRON OF HONOUR

The matron of honour does not wear the same costume as the bridesmaids.

BRIDESMAIDS

Bridesmaids should be allowed a say in the choice of dress and should wear the chosen attire and head-dress all day and evening.

It is usual for the bridesmaids to be allowed to keep their dresses and accessories after the wedding regardless of the purchaser.

PAGE BOYS

Velvet suits or kilts look very smart.

TRANSPORT

REQUIREMENTS

To Church
Bride's mother) separate
Bridesmaids   ) vehicle
Bride and giver-away

To Reception
Bride and groom
Attendants
Parents of the bride and groom

From Reception
Bride and groom

IDEAS
Car(s)	- Rolls Royce
	- Daimler
	- Limousine
	- Jaguar
	- Mercedes
	- Bentley
	- Vintage
Vintage carriage	- Horse-drawn with coachman and full livery
Haywain	
Coach	
Bus	
Taxi	

Superstition

It is lucky for the bride to meet a black cat, lamb, dove or spider on the way to the church.

It is unlucky to pass a pig or a funeral procession.

It is good luck to meet a chimney sweep at a wedding as he is associated with fire, warmth, the hearth and home.

In days of old, the bride's father gave one of her shoes to the husband so that he, as 'master' could tap her with it.

Country brides fear the crowing of a cock after dawn on the wedding day.

It is worth bearing in mind the following:

- Quotations should be obtained;
- Assess the number of cars and chauffeur(s) needed;
- Decide on type, style and colour;
- Vehicle(s) should be examined for space, cleanliness;
- Deposit/cancellation policy should be checked;
- Final payment arrangements must be checked.

RINGS

· · · · · · · · · · · · · ·

The giving of a ring or the exchange of rings is considered to be the heart of the church marriage service. The ring(s) are blessed by the minister and placed on the finger as a token of the promises made. However, the law does not compel that a ring is given at the marriage ceremony; rings are a part of ritual and tradition. The earliest examples of wedding rings are Roman and were made of iron, representing the durability of marriage and a sign that a down-payment or contract had been made. A variety of metals and materials followed, including leather and reeds.

The completeness of the circle shows love flowing in a continuous stream. Two matching rings, one for the bride and one for the groom, suggest togetherness. Exactness of fit means harmony and perfection. Never taking rings off determines permanence.

Tradition
Placing the ring on the third finger of the left hand recalls the ancient Egyptian belief that the vein of love ran directly from the heart to the tip of the third finger.

Although it is legal to borrow a ring for the ceremony, it is usual to have a new ring for a wedding.

The wedding ring(s) can match other wedding jewellery, e.g. engagement ring. It is advisable to choose a ring slightly too loose rather than too tight to allow for growth of fingers. Eternity rings are traditionally given on the birth of the first child or on a wedding anniversary.

TYPE OF RINGS

Gold	%	Carat	Description
Pure gold		24	Very soft, heavy, very strong natural colour, very expensive and difficult to obtain
Gold	91.6	22	Soft, fairly heavy, strong colour, expensive and difficult to obtain
	75	18	Serviceable and most practical
	37.5	9	Most durable
White		9	
Platinum			White, the most costly metal of all

FLOWERS

· · · · · · · · · · · · · ·

Flowers may be fresh, dried or imitation silk.
Supplies may be obtained from florists or from
nurseries.

	Superstition
Red roses	*- I love you*
White flowers	*- Innocence*
Purple flowers	*- The blood of Christ*
Camellia	*- Gratitude*
Forget-me-not	*- True love*
Iris	*- Hidden message*
Lily	*- Majesty*
white	*- Purity*
pink	*- Talent*
Lily-of-the-valley	*- Happiness*
Mimosa	*- Sensitivity*
Orange blossom	*- Chastity*
Rose	*- Love*
Snowdrop	*- Hope*
Sweet pea	*- Pleasure*
Violet	*- Faithfulness*
Cyclamen	*- Diffidence*
Hydrangea	*- Boastfulness*
Larkspur	*- Fickleness*
Marigold	*- Grief*
Narcissus	*- Egotism*

BOUQUET

A flower bouquet should be freshly made but if dampened, covered with moist tissue and kept cool (not in the fridge), it will remain fresh for many hours.

After the wedding, flowers can be pressed and kept as a memento.

Alternatives to bouquets include a white prayer-book, Bible, parasol, pomander, or Dorothy bag with drawstring.

CHURCH AND RECEPTION

Flowers for the church and reception are the crowning glory of the occasion and often reflect the colours in the bride's and her bridesmaids' headdresses.

If there are other weddings in church on the day, the cost of the flowers could be shared.

BUTTONHOLES

The groom, best man and fathers sometimes have double red carnations, but may choose white, pink or yellow ones, or even roses. Mothers wear single red or white buttonholes and may be given corsages, containing two or three large flowers.

It is worth bearing in mind the following:

- Availability of flowers should be checked;
- Capability of the florist should be assessed;
- Membership of a professional organisation can be checked;
- An itemised price list should be obtained;
- Delivery on the day or collection beforehand?
- Give full address.

GIFTS

· · · · · · · · · · · · · · ·

A wedding guest has no obligation to donate a gift nor should the bride's family feel that every present donor should be 'rewarded' with an invitation to the wedding.

If it is decided to make a list, less expensive items should be included so that guests do not feel 'blackmailed' into spending more than they can afford. Lists should be provided upon request and not before. Gifts for the home are still favourite and should be addressed to the bride at her home even if the donor has never met the bride.

Gifts should be sent in plenty of time before the wedding so that the bride may despatch thank-you notes before the event. The gifts may be displayed on the day for all to see. Gifts too large for display on the day should be represented by a card stating the present and donor(s). In the case of money, the amount should not be quoted.

Gifts given on the wedding day should be handed to a responsible person at the reception, perhaps the best man.

Gift List					
Item	Make	Model/colour design	Available from	Gift from	Thank you note sent

CANCELLATION OR POSTPONEMENT OF WEDDING

Prospective guests should be informed as soon as possible. In the case of cancellation, gifts should be returned immediately.

THE DAY

· ·

Tradition
A bride should not see her groom on the day of the wedding until they meet at the ceremony.

A timetable for the day should be compiled, stating who does what and giving contact numbers where appropriate.

Going-away attire and honeymoon provisions should be suitably placed at the reception.

The bride should do her hair first, followed by her make-up. She should then put on her dress, and finally swap her engagement ring to her right hand.

<u>*Superstition*</u>
It is considered good luck for the fully attired bride to glance in her mirror just once before leaving for her wedding; bad luck to return to look in the mirror after she has left the bedroom to commence her journey to the wedding.

The bridesmaids leave for the car, allowing mother and giver-away a few minutes with the bride. Mother joins bridesmaids in the car leaving father and daughter alone together.

Meanwhile the best man should be dressed and certain that he has the ring(s) in his waistcoat pocket and any other documentation, e.g. money for marriage fees (if not paid previously), travel tickets, passports and hotel reservations.

The groom may like to give the best man a sum of money to cover any out-of-pocket expenses that may be incurred during the day, e.g. tips.

—— *30 MINUTES*

Ushers arrive at the church, hand out service sheets and direct congregation to the pews, referring to their lists of close family.

Bride's family and friends sit on the left-hand side of the aisle (facing the altar) and the groom's guests on the right-hand side. Close family members are seated nearest the front.

—— *20 MINUTES*

Bell-ringing commences (if previously arranged), pealing until the ceremony starts.

—— *15 MINUTES*

Groom and best man arrive and stand in the front pew to the right of the central aisle, the best man on the groom's right. They sometimes wait in the vestry until a few minutes before the bride is due and then take up their positions.

—— *10 MINUTES*

Chief bridesmaid, bridesmaids, pages and bride's mother arrive and gather in the church porch.

—— *5 MINUTES*

Bride and giver-away arrive. The chief bridesmaid adjusts the bride's gown, veil and train and ensures that her engagement ring is on the right hand. Photographs may be taken.

The bride's mother enters the church. She is the last person to take her seat a few minutes before the ceremony starts and is accompanied by a male member of her family or an usher. She sits in the front pew to the left of the aisle. When the bride's mother takes her seat, this is a signal to the congregation that the ceremony is about to start.

The pages and bridesmaids form two columns at the main door through which the bride and the giver-away pass, or they may line up behind the bride.

The minister may wait for the procession at the chancel steps or, with the choir, greet the bride at the door and precede her up the aisle.

The organist changes tempo and begins the processional music. As soon as the bridal party enters the church, the groom moves from the

front pew to the right of the chancel steps, with
the best man at his right and a little behind him.
With the bride on the giver-away's right arm,
they proceed up the aisle. The attendants follow
in pairs (normally youngest in front).

The groom turns to greet the bride as she
proceeds slowly up the aisle. As the bride and
giver-away reach the groom at the chancel steps,
the groom and best man step slightly aside to the
right to form a line.

	Altar	
	Minister	
Bride		Groom
Bride's father		Best man
	Attendants	
PEWS		**PEWS**
Bride's		Groom's
relatives		relatives
and		and
friends		friends

The giver-away leads the bride to the groom's
left. The chief bridesmaid stands behind the
bride and slightly to her left. The chief
bridesmaid hands her bouquet to a bridesmaid
and steps forward. The bride turns and hands her
bouquet and gloves (if worn) to the chief
bridesmaid, who holds these until the bride has
signed the register. If there is no chief

bridesmaid, the bride's father takes the bouquet and hands it to his wife, who returns it to the bride in the vestry.

Some brides wear their engagement ring on their wedding finger right up to this point in the ceremony and choose this moment to change it to their right hand. Most will, however, have already made the switch when dressing for the wedding.

The chief bridesmaid may lift the bride's veil clear of her face, although the bride may do this herself during the ceremony, or in the vestry.

The service commences and lasts for about 35 minutes. This will have been rehearsed with the minister and all the attendants before the actual wedding day. The best man and bridal attendants remain in their places throughout the ceremony.

When the ceremony is concluded, the bride takes her husband's left arm, and the bridal attendants take up her train as she leaves the chancel. The bridal party follows the minister into the vestry. Others follow: bride's mother with groom's father; groom's mother with bride's father; and chief bridesmaid with best man.

The register is signed by the minister, the bride (using her maiden name probably for the last time if she chooses to take her husband's surname in future), the groom and two adult witnesses - usually the giver-away and the best man, but the chief bridesmaid (if she is of age) may sign.

A certificate is presented to the bride and remains, legally, her property. The groom claims the privilege of being the first to kiss his wife. Congratulations and good wishes are then showered upon the newly-married pair. The bride's bouquet is handed back to her by either the bridesmaid or the bride's mother. The groom offers his left arm to his bride, veil clear of her face. The attendants take up the bride's train.

The bride's father gives his arm to the groom's mother and the groom's father escorts the bride's mother.

The bridal party leaves the vestry and church in the following order: bride and groom, young attendants, chief bridesmaid, best man with other bridesmaids, bride's mother and groom's father, and groom's mother with bride's father.

The bride and groom should not be halted for congratulations as they proceed along the aisle. After all of the above have left the church, others may follow from the altar.

Superstition

Confetti, horseshoes and shoes are given to the couple as symbols of fertility. These are very ancient symbols believed to bring good luck. Horseshoes must be stored upright 'to keep in the luck'. Shoes symbolise authority and at one time they were thrown at newly-married couples for luck. Today, shoes are normally tied to the vehicle in which the couple leave for honeymoon.

Photographs are taken away from the church door, and finally, the best man ensures that the bride and groom take the first waiting car.

The second car is reserved for the bride's mother and groom's father, who are followed by the two remaining parents. The bridesmaids and guests follow either by way of their own transport or in a fleet of bridal cars.

The best man ensures that everyone has transport to the reception. He is the last to leave after settling fees but needs to arrive at the reception early.

Although the newly-weds are first to leave for the reception, the bride's parents (as host and hostess) need to arrive first.

The receiving line order at the reception should be: bride's mother, bride's father, groom's mother, groom's father, bride and groom, and attendants. If there are many guests, the reception line may be dispensed with and the guests briefly received by the bride and groom only.

Once all the guests have been offered a drink, the bride and groom are prompted by the best man to take their seats, if a meal is to be served. If there is to be a procession, the order should be: bride and groom, bride's father with groom's mother, groom's father with bride's mother, best man with chief bridesmaid, bridesmaids, pages, ushers, guests.

Speeches generally follow the meal. The usual order is the following:

- The best man acts as toastmaster and calls on the first speaker when he feels that the time is right.
- Giver-away or old and close friend of the bride proposes the health and happiness of the bride and groom.

Speech could include:

- How happy he and his wife have been bringing up their daughter;
- One or two short stories; welcome into the family of new son-in-law and groom's parents;
- Toast to bride and groom.

- Groom replies (on behalf of his wife and himself) thanking bride's parents, his parents and guests for their good wishes and gifts and all helpers who have made the reception a success.

Speech may include:

- Thank you to his parents for their care and attention to his upbringing and sacrifices they may have made;
- Tribute to his wife's parents;
- How he met bride;
- Future intentions to provide happiness;
- Thank you to the best man for his assistance;
- Reference to beauty of bridesmaids and thanking them; presents gifts for which they approach him.

- Groom proposes a toast to the bridesmaids.
- Best man replies on behalf of the bridesmaids and reads any messages received.
- The bride is seldom expected to make a speech but may do so if she wishes to thank her husband.

Tradition

It is traditional for the bride and groom to make the first cut in the cake together ceremonially. The groom places his hand over that of his bride. The bride places the knife point at the centre of the bottom cake tier. The groom places a hand over his wife's and slowly helps her to cut the cake. They may cut a slice and share it between them.

The bride and groom cut the cake, and then the caterers take over. Once it is cut the bridesmaids hand out slices of cake.

Tradition
Bridesmaids keep their slices and place them under their pillows that night in the belief that they will then dream of their own future husbands.

As the bride retires to change clothes (or when she leaves the reception for honeymoon), she throws her bouquet over her shoulder.

Tradition
It is said that the one who captures the bouquet can exspect to be the next bride.

Superstition
A bride should throw away every pin when removing her dress and veil or she will be unlucky.

The groom changes and awaits his wife. The best man hands over any travel documents. The groom may present his mother and mother-in-law with bouquets of flowers as they say good-bye.

<u>*Superstition*</u>
The first of the couple to purchase an item after the marriage is said to be the domineering partner!

The giver-away settles the hotel account. The guests should say good-byes to the host and hostess before leaving. The host, hostess and best man are the last to leave.

The bride's mother collects the remains of the cake, her daughter's clothes and checks that nothing is left behind by female guests. The best man ensures that messages are handed to the bride's mother to be kept for the bride upon her return from honeymoon. The best man collects the groom's clothes and checks that nothing is left behind by male guests. He collects gifts and transports them to the bride's parents' home.

SPEECHES

Hints

- Dress unobtrusively and avoid anything that jangles;
- Avoid embarrassing stories;
- Be careful of telling jokes;
- Be brief (two minutes is ample), appropriate and to the point;
- Plan;
- Write down speech on small cards organised

in small sections. Use bold headings and number the pages;
- Practise;
- During the speech refer to headings as memory-joggers; do not read the cards;
- Do not drink too much;
- Before commencing, take a deep breath;
- Stand comfortably and still, with feet slightly apart;
- Hold something in your hand or hold your hands behind back;
- Speak slowly and clearly;
- Look at the audience in general; do not stare at one person;
- Vary speed and voice level.

AFTERWARDS

GROOM'S CLOTHES

The best man returns hired attire if appropriate.

CAKE

Small slices of cake are sent by the bride's mother to those who were unable to attend on the day.

GIFTS

Shortly before the newly-weds return, the bride's parents should take the gifts to their daughter's new home.

HONEYMOONERS' RETURN

Tradition
The husband should carry his wife over the threshold of their new home in order to bring good fortune in their future life.

EXPENSES

The husband reimburses the best man any out-of-pocket expenses incurred at the wedding.

THANK-YOU NOTES

The bride sends 'thank-you' notes to gift donors

and acknowledgement notes to message senders. These must be sent promptly on return from honeymoon if not dealt with beforehand. They should be handwritten.

WILLS AND INSURANCE

It is advisable to make new wills as soon as possible. If the husband makes no provision for life insurance, his wife could suffer financially.

Many documents will have to be changed, e.g. passports, driver's licence, bank accounts, etc.

PRESS ANNOUNCEMENT FOLLOWING THE WEDDING

The bride's parents are responsible for publishing an announcement (if desired) under 'Marriages' in the classified section. The usual wording is as follows:

MR SAMUEL SOUTH AND MISS NEL NORTH
The marriage took place on ... at the Church of ..., of Mr Samuel South, only son of Mr and Mrs Sidney South of Southton and Miss Nel North, younger daughter of Mr and Mrs Nigel North of Northton.

INDEX

• • • • • • • • • • • • •